CHESTER

OF CHESTNUT SQUARE

LC TOBEY   STEVIE GLEW   ANNE ROYER

ILLUSTRATED BY:
LOGAN LARSEN & CARISSA PELOUCH
LAY-OUT BY: MADISON DOAK

PUBLISHER LC TOBEY

Thank you for purchasing this book.
All proceeds benefit the following
non-profits:

Chestnut Square Historical Village
www.chestnutsquare.org

Arts and Music Guild
www.artsandmusicguild.org

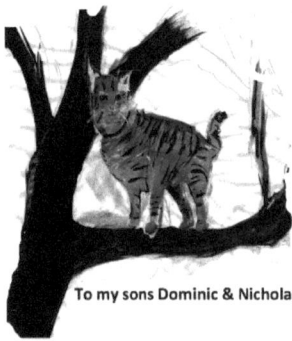

To my sons Dominic & Nicholas Demichina

Printed in United States of America
ISBN 978-0-615-73550-4

One day a friendly silver striped cat, looking for a new home, wandered into Chestnut Square Historical Village.

He found a large yellow house
with a pleasing porch where he
laid down to take a lazy nap.

"Wake up, Sleepyhead! It's a beautiful day at Chestnut Square!" said a big, orange and black Monarch butterfly flapping around the gray cat's ears.

The cat looked at the pretty butterfly and purred, "Chestnut Square? What's that?"

"It's a beautiful historic village that many of us call home,"explained the butterfly. "I'm Darcy. C'mon, I'll give you a tour."

They began at the Visitor's Center, where the cat admired the elegant fountain.

Pausing in front of the little white church, she continued, "This is the wedding chapel. Many happy people have been married here." Darcy fluttered around the cat excitedly.

Hearing the din of faraway voices, the cat perked his ears and asked, "Oh my, what's all that noise?"

"That's coming from the Farmers Market," explained Darcy.

"Farmers Market? I haven't been to a farmers market since I was a little kitten in the country." Licking his lips, he asked, "Do they have treats?"

"Of course," said Darcy, "and fresh fruits and vegetables." "I smell bread!" whispered the cat. "It's straight out of the oven," replied Darcy.

The gray cat & butterfly moved quietly toward the crowded market.

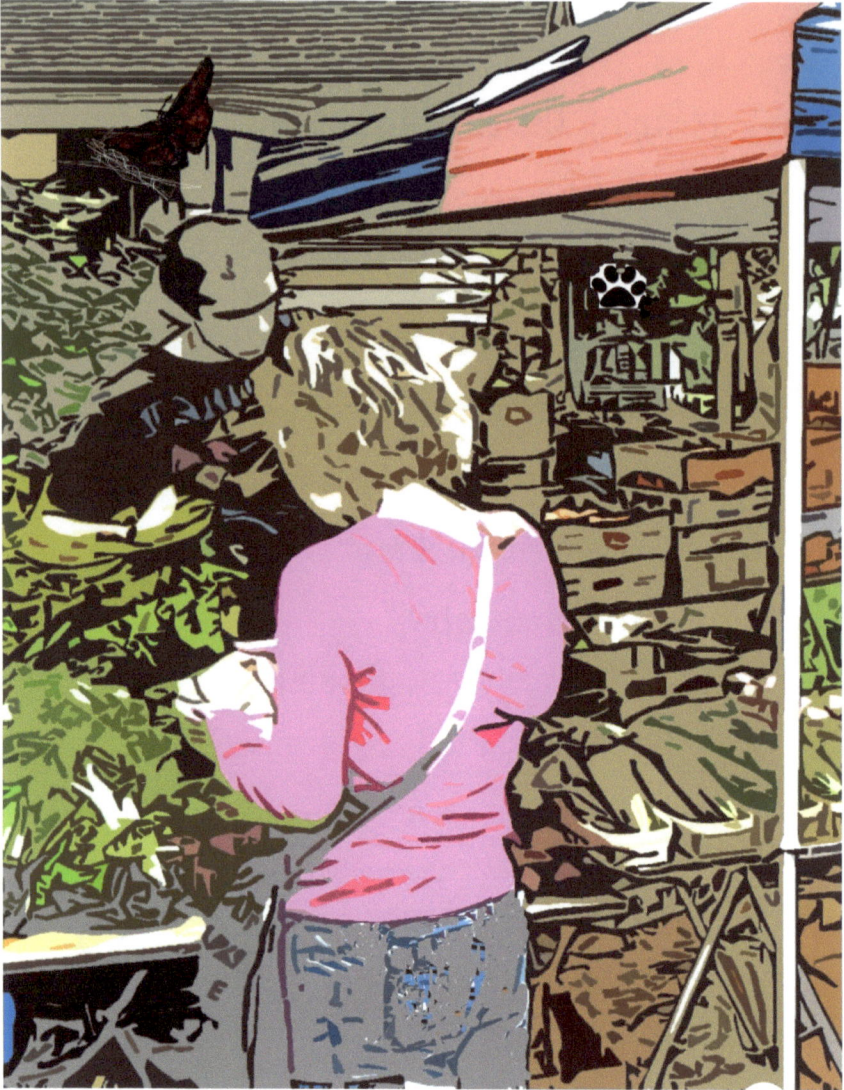

Can you find Darcy the butterfly at
the Farmers Market?

Now let's try and find Chester's hiding place!

Here you go, little fella. You've been so helpful today, we would like you to stay. We'll name you "Chester."

"Oooohhh, kitty snacks. Yummy..... I like this lady!"

After a full day of greeting people at the Farmers Market, the friendly gray cat had made many friends.

He met the Director of Chestnut Square. She decided to name him "Chester," and hoped he would stay.

Armed with his new name, Chester introduced himself to every creature he met. A curious dog by the name of Bellamy gave Chester a sniff, to which the cat gave a hearty, "Welcome to Chestnut Square! I'm Chester!"

That day, Chester met all the animals that live at Chestnut Square. He met two goats named Collin and McKinney. They shared a little history with him. Dart, the dragonfly, joined the conversation. Off in the distance, a disrespectful mockingbird named Sydney tried to interrupt the new friends.

Every morning to the delight of
visitors, Chester lounges on the
countertop of the Dixie Store. He
is always happy to be rewarded
with a bowl of treats.

Then he would
find Dart, and enjoy
a friendly game of
"Cat & Dragonfly."

At the Faires House,
Chester stood at
attention as a volunteer
hung the flag for the
day.

Next, it was off to work. At his computer in the Director's office, Chester spread the news of his new home to friends across the Internet. ("Like" Chester of Chestnut Square on Facebook and join his fan page!)

Later that evening Chester
was invited to his first Board
of Directors meeting, which
he proudly led.

After a long day of making new
friends and having fun, Chester fell
asleep in a warm, cozy chair located
in the Director's office.

"Before our story ends, Darcy,
I would like to thank all the people
who told it for us," said Chester.

"Stevie Glew gave us words,
Logan Larsen and Carissa Pelouch
painted our portraits. Madison
Doak worked on the scans and
layouts. Then there was Anne Royer
who guided the young artists. We
must not forget the staff at Chestnut
Square and The McKinney Animal
Hospital who take of us!", exclaimed
Chester.

"Thank you everyone!" added Darcy.

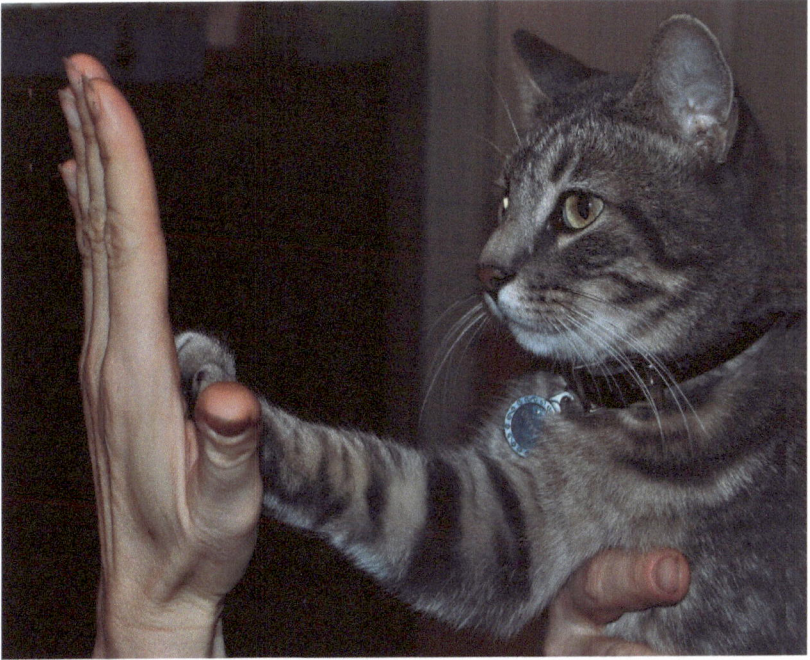

"High five," said Chester,
"Chestnut Square is my
forever home."

Madison Doak, Carissa Pelouch, Stevie Glew & Logan Larsen.

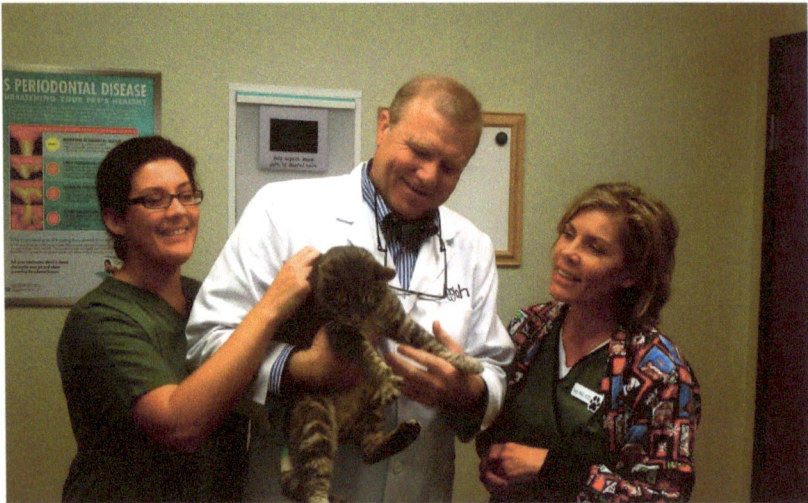

Dr. Bloomer & Staff with Chester.

Chester with his Chestnut Square Family:

Front Row: Kim Ducote, Wedding Coordinator
Terri Monk, Education Coordinator

Back Row: Elaine Bay & Patricia Nall, Grounds
Alice Yeager, Volunteer Coordinator
LC Tobey, Bookkeper
Cincy Johnson, Director of Chestnut Square

www.ingramcontent.com/pod-product-compliance
Lightning Source LLC
Chambersburg PA
CBHW041803040426
42448CB00001B/30